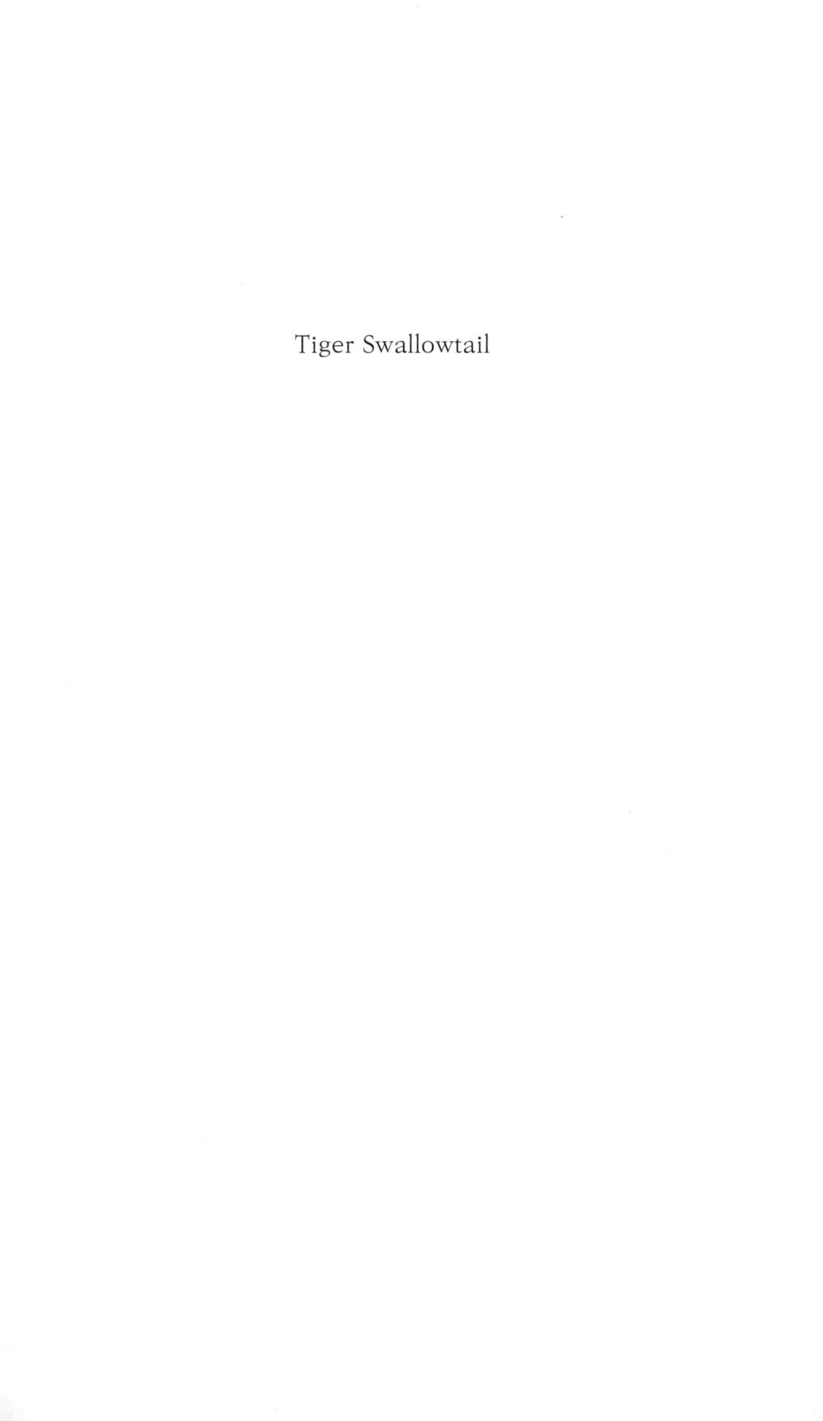

Tiger Swallowtail

Contents

Tiger Swallowtail

My Loneliest High Place

I've now reached a place from which I can no longer walk forward.
While the sea tries to bite off a hard crag
With its brilliant white teeth,
The horizon, hidden behind dark clouds, stays invisible.
—Hydrangeas are laying down their colors.
As I stop walking and gasp for breath
At a point where I can no longer walk forward,
I haven't yet developed wings, and I will not do so in the future.
Faraway, separating the waves
Is a lonely fishing boat, hiding its speed.

It does not look to be going forward,

But instead throwing its entire body into the unknown.

At a place where winds also depart, after erasing illusions,

At this loneliest high place of mine,

I decide to turn back, as the way forward has vanished.

As I stumble through my steps again,

I decide to illuminate them in deep black under the sun,

Like the sea abruptly rising in the midst of sobbing,

Like that void in which the sound of breathing

subsides

And the darkness grows ever deeper.

Rain. Is. Shattered.

These days rain falls in pieces.
I'm not talking about the other side of clouds
Clinging to a windowpane. I mean a time
When rain falls like dust, instead of
To form dark depths, has arrived.
It began not long ago.
We killed tranquility and silence and transformed them into streets.
We lit time and have been operating machines with it.
Ever since, rain has been falling in pieces.
That is why, when it begins to rain,
We hurriedly close the windows, as if we heard an alarm bell.

It is only trees and flowers, deprived of fields,
That now endure it.
After the rain, we have become more and more thirsty,
And brooks have lost their murmurings.
Even our language has been crumbling
And is leaving us bit by bit.

Let's Set the Forests Free

Let's finally set those forests free.
Instead of blocking them with cars,
Instead of cutting them off, joint by joint, with saws,
Let's set them free, so they can give birth to hearts.
So they rock and nestle the rain and winds,
Which, in turn, become springs, flow down and down,
Thousands of miles, and finally turn into the vast sea,
Let's set them free from humans.
Let's set them free for humble villages.
For baskets about to be born, for rough hardened

knuckles,

For the fluttering, quivering butterflies, and the diligent beaks of woodpeckers,

Let's now set them free,

Let's set the forests free,

Free from large desks,

And comfortable houses.

And, finally, let's install forests as our new lords

And let human beings become their foolish subjects.

Spring

The brookside is gradually turning lime green,
And the path crawling over the lowish mountain ridge
Dazzlingly bends away like a golden serpent.
While the sunlight splits open the murky sky and brightly pours down,
The field is tanning its forearms
And taking off its thick outer clothes.

Along the nape, in no time, perspiration is streaming down.

Let's Write Poems

Let's write poems when feeling hurt.

Let's write poems when feeling lonely.

Let's write poems when feeling sad in our impoverished hearts.

And let's compose poems when feeling left behind.

When feeling overwhelmed by the affair of living in this world,

When the moon does not rise,

When creeks become leaner and leaner,

When you feel secretly sad,

As our children have grown,

Let's also write poems. Although writing poems

We might feel more hurt and lonely,

We might feel twinkling starlight even harder to bear,
Let's still write poems.
Only the time when we write will be shining,
And that shining will make dew drops
On a spider's web stay,
So let's still write poems—and when we do so,
Although we might become poverty, might become solitude,
Might become raindrops,
Although, at best, we might become the light in the eyes of a squirrel,
And although only the embers might continue to throb.

Swallows

I still sometimes remember the swallows that have now vanished:

The way they would soar, after flying low and near—almost grazing—the ground;

Or the way the chicks would chirp,

Thrusting their red throats upward and welcoming their mother.

The dusk when Mother returned home after a day's labor

At a bokchoy farm on a riverside almost three miles away

Was the moment my life would brighten,

But those swallows were driven far away,

And I went out into this cruel world.

It has been five years today

Since young swallows who had just begun to flap their wings were left to drown in the cold sea.*

* On April 16, 2014, A ferry, the Sewol, sailing toward Jeju Island from Incheon, sank in front of Jindo Island, Jeollanam-do. Among its 476 passengers were 325 students from Danwon High School, located Ansan, Gyeonggi-do, on their way to a field trip in Jeju Island. Of 304 dead and missing, 250 were these high-school students. The South Korean government and Coast Guard did not save them.

Standing at the Horizon

Every step forward becomes the last extremity.
When, away from old friends,
I breathe in the desolation
That blows from an irrevocable direction,
I stand again face to face with the horizon.

Whenever a worm labors to give birth to eggs
Where the new sun rises,

Like a lightning rod calling to the lightning,
The time that I left behind
Sets fire to dry fields,
And the ruins blow a different life into them.

Standing on the horizon,

I set down both flowers and rocks.

I also send away creeks and starlight.

The horizon is ruins that make ruins shine!

I am silently watching

Only the darkness without a border.

A Typhoon's Lesson

Finally, a violent gale arose,
And trees bobbed up and down, as if about to be uprooted.

Whenever their trunks bent, about to break,
Their fruits fell and pattered,
And dark clouds receded and returned like waves.

At this moment the leaves feel
Their roots more deeply than ever.

When the winds depart,
After leaving the truth of solitude born,
Only after memories pour down, like waterfalls,

Time, made simpler, has arrived.

Although the winds have left and the earth remains,
A Sadness different from that of yesterday has come,
And a poverty different has been created.

Looking at the darkening sky,
The color of the remaining fruits undulates.

A Time of a Precipice

Blindly, we're heading toward a precipice.

Someone blames the fog, and says,

It's our fate: we have no other choice but to keep going, even though we cannot see.

And we don't have to get out a compass for directions,

Because, after all, that compass is not ours.

Whether rivers are still flowing through the places we've left,

Whether the void is beating like the hearts of seagulls flying far away—

They are of no consequence,

Because they are what we have left behind.

We don't even know why this is the case. Buildings grow taller

And roads continue to spread. Night becomes day,

And day reproduces as day.

It is being indefinitely refilled.

The road we've taken so far must be hidden, disappear,

Or lie inertly on a display stand,

Because we're now heading toward a precipice.

Sometimes ecstasy, and last night solitude,

Entered inside, after breaking a window.

But as soon as the sun rises, the front door opens automatically.

This design was made a very long time ago.

We're heading toward a precipice, clutching our beastly hearts.

Although we sometimes stop and look back,

Although in the afternoon we sometimes look at flowers along the road,

We are going on like a winter tree

With broken branches—like the shadow of a pigeon,

We are going forward limping

On the road where we may turn into a precipice.

It is the time of a precipice—

A time when we can roll our bodies like pebbles, but only after we become a precipice.

It is the time of a precipice.

Spring Snow

Were it to snow, it should snow day and night for at least ten days.

Were it to snow, it should snow at least until it buries us up to our waists.

It should at least stop the buses, and even erase the snowmen.

We are now gradually passing out of the human world.

Make sure to wear a mask, because viruses are roaming around.

But they are what we threw away,

Not monsters that suddenly appeared.

That is why the snow flurries, now pouring down instead of sunbeams, are pale.

When the sun sets, the road will become icy,

And, not knowing what to do, the cars will

Turn around, plop down, and be at a loss—

I hope that death will not knock at the front door yet—

Because anything faster than the speed of our walking is itself a lethal weapon.

Perhaps the building under construction next to my office is almost completed now,

Because I see the tower crane being disassembled.

While I find the words, which are not descending in my heart,

Scarier than viruses,

Clouds that didn't show up when I called

Abruptly pour down onto the earth.

If they must fall, they should completely muffle both love and waiting.

They should pour down until what is tall and big

Flattens and becomes desolate.

Shadows

Despite my desperate pleading not to cut them down,
I find the trees near the children's playground have become ghastly today.
June is the time the sun comes near us, after rolling up its sleeves,
But, claiming they cut them so close
So the small branches do not break off and hurt the children,
City Hall officials seem to find complaints from me, who appears to be hung over, unwelcome.
No, they definitely find them unwelcome.
I now seem to feel a fishy smell and hear
The sound of raindrops—I am growing older—

From the tone of voice and choice of words my interlocutor chooses.

As the hot summer approaches,

Indeed, I feel stifled even before its arrival.

If the trees are left only with trunks, since all the branches have been cut,

Typhoons will not visit us, and the faces of creeks will not swell

From crying during the rainy season.

But because bureaucracy is like a too-dense forest,

I remain hung over, although the sun is high in the sky.

Once was a time that spirits lived, attached to the

trees,

Although I cannot remember the prayers people said in front of them.

Even cut down, the branches are bound to grow back,

So I wonder what you're so worried about, sir.

The distance between there and here is so extreme.

In that distance, only my pessimism grows.

The sound of an electric-powered saw does not stop, even during our arguments,

And one after another, the shadows are being severed.

Daytime Moon

To a degree, my body belongs to the jujube tree in front of my house.

It is also the sorrowful sigh of my mother,

Yesterday's fierce gusts,

And the letter I wrote last night

Among the rocks,

Through which a sip of spring water

I met in a thirsty forest

Has been trickling down,

And, at last, reached me.

As even in the crater of a volcano a tiny living organism is born,

So the sunlight, which reaches the river and lies down on it,

Makes the expression of grains of sand spread on the riverbed.

And your shade again becomes my body.

Although, during this winter without a single snowflake,

Deserts are approaching, with heavy footsteps,

At 4 pm, the moon rises again,

Alone and lonely.

Don't be sick.

Even if our songs may not reach

Beyond the horizon,

The moon, trembling,

Achieves a smile, as much as it puts on darkness.

Cremation

Is it only a disaster

That can stop us now? When belated snow stop,

Shy spring breezes finally begin to blow,

And creeks become a little clearer.

My voice has been too loud.

I'll have to become a little smaller,

And much darker, like a valley.

I should have bought Mother a small patch of black field

Even if I had to borrow from the bank.

Even while the streets are filled with stillness half the time,

Noises, like waves, from automobiles do not cease.

While what can really stop us is solitude with
dreams,
Can a baby, still covered in its mom's blood,
Begin to form fists
From the shriek of those felled trees?
I will no longer wander in the face of tragedy.
I will snap outwardly growing words into pieces
To throw into a furnace.
From the cooler side of the room, beansprouts
will
Murmur overnight in a jar,
And fig trees
Will gradually ripen in my dreams.

There Is Nothing But Flowers

While flowers bloom, there is nothing but flowers.
There are neither butterflies nor bees.
There are neither the faces that I miss, nor the souls
That are fluttering together in the winds.

While flowers bloom, there is nothing but flowers.
Nothing but dark glances looking at nothing but the flowers.
Nothing but the memory of cries
From brown-eared bulbuls and time deserted.

While flowers bloom, there is nothing but flowers.
Nothing but lonely dreams calling to empty

hearts.

Nothing but the sadness of living amidst disasters.

Nothing but a river that hasn't been crossed yet.

While flowers bloom, there is nothing but flowers.

Nothing but flowers, nothing but flowers···

Nothing but footsteps pausing only momentarily,

Nothing but the faraway mountains, finally visible.

Nothing but the yearning that calls the faraway mountains to come and lie nearer.

The Road Not Taken

The road not taken is always
The road left behind.
It's the void that cabbage butterflies, used to flying above cabbage fields,
Left behind, or a path
That slowly followed cows, together with the lapping sound of a stream. It is neither
The road yet to be taken, nor
The road shining under the streetlights
You look at momentarily, while flipping through a book in the middle of night.
It is a bent but pitch-black road,
A road filled only with Spanish needles.
The road not taken is always

An invisible road, a road on which you begin again

At the moment when your lungs are entirely filled with cold wind

On your way back, after resolutely confirming

That the light inside a window was turned off.

It is the road on the side of the mountain behind your house, one that you climbed

After returning from the river, to which you went, but could not become a river;

The road toward a broad flat rock, where the glow of the setting sun lingered for a long time.

The road not taken is

A road where aches from a daylong hoeing

Are crawling all over your body;

The road on which your heels are reddened;

The road where only songs roam like ghosts;

The road faintly visible at the end of crying.

The True Identity of Waves

It seems like these waves were raised not by the wind,

But by underwater creatures.

The wind is probably just nodding affirmatively,

While differently shaped fish,

Faintly quivering water plants, or words chattered

By eyeless worms

Raise and set down those fluttering waves.

Otherwise, I don't think it's possible for that enormous soul

To flow, while crumpling us.

Although the winds come from invisible places,

Underwater creatures yield to them,

Just to momentarily blind us,

And to have us discharge what's inscribed in our bodies.

It seems that those waves

Are somehow raised up by billions of lives.

They seem like outstretched hands,

Inviting even the sunlight to a dance along with them.

Again

An old tree no longer grows taller,

But begins to vacate its body.

It also bends its body,

So that birds can live in it, winds can alight,

And village children can climb up.

To spread to every corner of the village

The truth that it can no longer grow taller,

Its soul changes.

Growing forever and ever is

Not possible even by God.

That's why God shut his mouth

Like a fine clear sky.

Even trees cannot grow to reach the clouds.

As rivers return to the parched land

As spring rain,

And pass through the rocks

And start towards themselves again,

Trees also stop growing taller,

Instead growing smaller and lighter.

Only leaves give birth again to

Dazzling breaths,

Murmuring, susurrant songs.

The Voice of a Creek

— For the Spirit of Mr. Kim Jong-chul

1

When I proposed that we visit a wounded river together,
You responded: *Let's have a meal and a drink.*
There, in a metropolitan alley, I don't remember what we talked about.
I only remember the laughter
You gave me, while walking together after the meal.
The light from my realization that you liked my homeliness a little
Entered my body at a not-too-high voltage.
I had been too slow-witted—

An utterly ignorant, dim self.

The moment a river flowed out of my mouth

And you dropped a meal and wine into it—

To me, that moment was like a work of construction.

No, it was like an earthquake.

You baptized me with fire with your writing,

And a baptism by immersion with words and laughter.

They were an underground spring, gushing out,

Like a creek slowly soaking parched rice paddies.

And a young rice seedling

Brightened a little.

2

During the time when I had no father,

To my memories in which I tried to drive away my father as far as possible,

You asked, *Have you traveled abroad?*

I said, *I don't even have a passport.*

You responded, *My, what a country bumpkin!*

Knock, knock, you knocked on my door,

And proposed becoming friends.

You asked, *Why did you leave early yesterday?*

Were you upset?

I said, *No, I had another engagement.*

You said, I wonder since when I worry about you

all.

Make sure to survive!

How the young rice seedling, cut off from water, will grow from now on—

Nobody now knows.

They say the voice that often collected us and forced us to sit down has gone.

But today I flung down my black clothes while putting them on.

Don't say something unnecessarily difficult,

Just write so that your mother can understand.

I have continued to torture myself with those words of yours.

You said, *although we all have to leave when the*

time comes, as long as we're alive,

*Let's continue to struggle, love, and long.**

But this poem that I'm writing today is not an ele-

gy.

It is the dim and dark interior

Of the poverty without a home to return to,

Which I could not show you while you were alive.

* When I showed Kim Jong-chul my essay "Rainy Season," he sent me a reply, whose entire text is as follows: "Thank you. I'd like to urge you to continue to write essays like this. Don't say something unnecessarily difficult. It seems that to frankly share the sadness and pain from losing, as we continue to lose our hometowns, is what literature is all about—while, although we all have to leave when the time comes, as long as we're alive, continuing to struggle, love, and long." The time stamp showed that it was sent at 20:47 on June 24, 2020. It was early the next morning that he passed away at Baeksasil Valley in Buam-dong, Jongno-gu, Seoul. Although he jokingly said that he was being paid back by noise because he had hated noise all his life, it really feels like he was being murdered by noise.

As you continue to complain that you hear the sound of the airplane,

This is one of my attempts at recitation for you.

I trust that you have now shaken off the airplane noise,

And will come back as the sound of murmuring creeks.

All right, I get it.

Although we're still dim,

We, remaining here, will add water to the drying creeks, sip by sip.

See you again soon.

3

Don't make a fuss.

When human beings get older, they all become ill,

And then they die.

Tiger Swallowtail

1

The rainy season does not end; the sea is boiling;
Alarmed, glaciers are crashing down, and continents burn.

While this could all be because the forests have been deeply felled,
In semi-basement rooms, mold is gradually
Creating deeper and deeper jungles.

While wearing face masks, no matter how much sanitizer
You spray on hands, something more to be ex-

posed seems to remain.

(Now silence is a vice,

And you would like to hear anybody say anything.)

In the rain, cicadas, unable to finish crying,

Are dumped on the road,

While, after the rain, occasionally, between clouds,

The glow of the setting sun, like a fall sky,

Is beautiful, looking down at the city.

The face of the earth is that infinite.

2

Looking back, you find a person from whom almost all of her body's time has been drained.

After putting down a hoe, wagon, and rumination of a cow,

Unable to stretch her bent back,

She silently stares at the faraway field across.

Although, together with her crumbling house,

She has endured forced labor,

Wars,

Fleeings,

And separations,

She can still hear her young daughter's voice,

Whom she lost to the river risen from the monsoon rain.

Her submerged cry

Is flowing down to the creek.

Although a dusk descended on and darkened the field

When she was crying, leaning against a stone wall,

Having put a worn-out straw bag in the middle of the yard,

Time is running fast

Along the road widened since then.

They say torrential rain will start up again in the evening.

3

Might the river overflow tonight?
Perhaps it will only hang a lot of trash
Along the riverbank.
While, hiding behind the sound of the rain,
I'm secretly unloading
All the sadness that has been accumulating,
The front door is opened abruptly, and, folding
A wet umbrella, my child takes off her backpack
and flings it down.
When, amid the lights—neither one nor many—
Of the houses that lost neighbors,

Torrential rain pours down again,

Cars that could not manage to go,

Don't know what to do, rubbing their bodies.

Hope is also gradually dimming.

A worn-out fan, in order to dry wet laundry,

Brings a wet breeze.

4

Mother, I hear that deep in the valleys

Trees talk to you;

That leaves shine even when there is no light;

That, when you feel that beaming,

Your soul opens with a creaking sound;

That, although collapsing as a wreck, we seem to bid eternal farewell,

We become at last naked,

Just as the underground water passes through rocks

And flows into

The breathing sound of dark worms.

There perhaps

We can begin again?

From the direction of a crumbling hamlet,

A tiger swallowtail flew toward me, then led me

In the direction of Prajna Hall. There

I collapsed briefly and cried.

Over my body, prostrated face down,

The sound of rain I heard for the first time approached.

They were quiet footsteps.

5

From the mouth of a cow plowing the fields

White foam drips down

Onto the weed-grown, fallow lands.

The sun in midair.

Colors of Darkness
— After Seeing the Exhibit "Flower Garden" by Cha Kyu Sun

There are colors even in darkness:

Flowers, rocks,

Peaks, trees,

Even kisses are colors of darkness.

Darkness flows down and blooms, at the same time; it also pours down,

While staying inside; sometimes it flies around animatedly

Above our heads for about a fortnight.

Mountains are darkness's upheaval,

Valleys are its pause—Would you believe

Even a language exists in darkness?

Silence is a stream flowing in our hearts,

And the darkness, which we have discarded

through our lives,

Is indeed our sea.

That the life, yawning at birth,

Covers, spreads, embraces, and faints

Is entirely the darkness's work of construction.

Therefore, we're petals scattered everywhere—

Or like a rubber ball floating and bobbling

In darkness, like winds,

Like a low wall

That does not catch the winds.

Toward the Direction of Daybreak

A road newly taken is always fraught with fear.
From a valley filled with a fog,
Hitherto unheard sound reaches you, and the sound of groaning
From a body bumped and broken against a rock
Wrings your heart.
A road newly taken
Is a road always taken for the first time.
A throbbing heart means that rocks on a slope
Are rumbling down toward me and crashing.
Fresh buds of a Mongolian oak have sprouted between my fingers,
While clouds have been curling in white.
As if the road newly taken wants

To offer me a different kind of darkness,
The glow of the setting sun has just reached my smallest toe.
Like the raindrops falling on the bean leaves,
Like the song sung by icicles under the diffusing sunlight,
The road newly taken is one on which I am being erased.
A road where I walk, laugh, and grow old—
Like petals reddening amid the winds,
The road newly taken
Is always whirling dizzyingly,
Breathing and panting,
And twisting its back toward the direction where

day is breaking.

Resurrection

We keep going, as rivers flow.
If we stop, we're dead. Even if we don't stop,
We will die.
Even amid abruptly pouring torrential rain, there is sadness,
There are breaths gasping for the air,
And there are fields prodding themselves.
And therefore raindrops call and touch one another,
And split, and finally become rivers.
I believe this is love—
Neither misery, nor resentment,
But resurrection.
Carrying the memories of valleys,

Rivers flow toward the sea, while growing reeds,
And recreating the gestures of water birds.
This is the power of death.
However, it's a music that still cannot be heard,
Because the sound of someone's calling
Is only faintly heard through the clouds.
We keep going like the rivers that forever overturn their bodies.
Stars will rise behind us.
We can accept even pitch-black time.
Perhaps then,
The music could be heard.
I mean the time when death smiles brightly.
Together with the center of the hardships, which

have never not been hardships,

We keep going.

Jujube Tree

While I was fighting with a hoe in a crumbling house
Against a man wielding a knife in my dream,
The jujube tree outside must have been so harassed by the typhoon
That even its branches have turned haggard.
The tree that sends out its leaves last,
And leaves the firmest seeds
Bobbed with all its might whenever the winds blew.
The jujube tree is still bending its body
To the lingering winds, as if to say
That nightmares are dreams had by only hardened souls.

And meanwhile, with whom am I now
Listening to the sound of the winds?
We are beings whose roots have become rotten.
So we undertake even the affair of loving
As if assuming a heavy burden.
Even if we don't go far, even if we can't imagine
Something enormous,
There are shining eyes and sounds nearby—

How deep the world is!

A Pickaxe and a Donkey

Although we can no longer see dirt-encrusted footsteps
Returning home together with the glow of the setting sun,
A pickaxe and a donkey
Still remain in our souls.
As earthworms emerge and dance on a rainy day
Even during when mountains
Are burning, bridges collapsing, and the ice continent melting,
The pickaxe and donkey are shining brightly, like the void after a typhoon.
Even when everyone closes their eyes, saying it's too late,

The pickaxe cultivates the earth from dawn,

And the donkey, after finishing its poor meal, looks at the road ahead.

Here, where everyone is discarded in the evening,

Although automatic machines and gigantic trucks go at breakneck speed,

A pickaxe is wiping away sweat somewhere,

And a thirsty donkey is dipping its head into a water bucket.

The reason the long neck of a heron,

as it dips its ankles in the stream, is quietly shining

Is that a pickaxe and donkey

Are still holding onto us tightly,

Because they are blowing pitch-black darkness into our souls,

And because love begins because of it.

Half Moon

Once, when I was 15, the half moon
Bit off the rest of my heart.
I happened to secretly see, while bathing,
The moon with its feet in the river—
Was it perhaps late summer in the field?
It was a time when in my dream
Water scales were sprouting all over my body
While I was wandering among water plants.
—The downstream was in the west.
Like the light of a train passing the railway tracks,
I wished to float faraway alone downstream
To become the sea,
But the half moon called me back over and over again.

However, when the half moon was hidden behind the clouds
And one could hear only a dog barking on a narrow path along a ravine,
I finally decided to leave.
Since I could no longer see the half moon,
Because the world had become too bright,
I lived without remembering the half moon for a long time,
But the moon, as if to tell me it had never forgotten me,
Is illuminating my indigent memory.
Although it will leave tomorrow night, faraway,
It tells me that it will come back some day,

And become the half of my soul;

That I have to wait.

Snowstorm

I don't know whether it is light or shade
That's streaming down from your eyes.
It seems that we will arrive at the unknown,
Only after we have lived through all the low and miserable moments.
How steep the hills are; where the sun rises;
Or what memories redden the moon—
I don't know, but I seem to know; and when I seem to know, darkness descends.
It's a place we cannot reach
Through a prayer during which our knees turn into fossils.
It is the pain we gain only after plowing the field,
Or the dream that comes to us

Only after we cry with all our body
Alone at the riverbank.
It could be like being on the bridge swinging
Because of kisses with nowhere to go.
At a place where we cannot stay long,
We hear the clamor of a painful grief again.
Just to reach such a place,
We walk overnight,
And leave our hearts at the reservoir that loves the sunlight.
We are just a drop of water,
A spider wrapped in a standstill,
And the ankle of a soaring bird.
We are a trough of deepening low pressure, about

to burst and pour down;

And the snowstorm passing

From peak to peak.

Winter Valley

One day when large snowflakes fall,
I should wake up in the morning
To board a train panting and crossing over the pass.
A steep life, where you can't go fast, even if you want to,
Is the supreme bliss.
Things left and gone will fill your view
As snowflakes the size of your fists.
They are probably a different world
Approaching a soul that has transferred to a different time.
The valley will become deeper,
And the path will be as quiet as a frozen river.

Memories floating up from it

Will no longer be mine.

They will be the white river flowing between you and me,

Or the look in the eyes of a baby elk,

Left alone and turning around to look back, on its way up the mountain ridge.

The dream that I have never let go of

And also love continue to cut me down—

The me of yesterday;

That dream and love let me forever slide and tumble;

And tell me to let go of all the luggage I've been carrying,

To let them go like stations I passed by;

To become a stream melting and flowing

In pursuit of the dream of becoming penniless;

To flow down the fields that I see for the first time,

Looking around.

POET'S NOTE

Throughout my life, I've been wondering what I can do with poems. And, since sometime ago, I've found myself walking alone and wondering what poems can become. I feel like this solitary walking could become more frequent, and I am not at all afraid of it, even if I end up walking endlessly.

Could there be a fable in which a donkey becomes a tiger swallowtail?

THE POET'S ESSAY

For Poems to Become "Something" in Reality on Their Own

I have long thought about how poems can change our actual world. Although it's not right to condemn this idea for being utilitarian, I also don't deny that such an idea can fall into the trap of utilitarianism, in some situations, or if one thinks solely about it. From a different angle, we can say that it's more dangerous to try not expecting any "trap" on the path of poems—such an expectation might itself be a state in which one has already been entrapped. Yet isn't the state where you are aware or afraid of a possible trap also a poetic state of mind? If we believe that poems are the work of getting rid of falsehood, from both within and outside of what's visible, and searching for and creating true identities, our expectation of possible traps in this work can indeed make our poems stronger.

These days, reality exists in our minds as fragmented. Although understanding reality in its totality has long gone, this does not mean the world itself exists as fragmented though. It's we who understand the world as fragmented, and the external condition that makes us understand the world in such a way is our reality. If poems always originate from our concrete lives, it is natural for them to be responsive to fragmented reality, despite the axiom that poems are meant to change our reality. However, poems need to fight back against this reality—this is what I'd like to call as poems becoming "something" in reality on their own.

This becoming is a sort of exploration. For poems to become "something" real is not a strategy of giving up on changing reality, but instead a transformation necessary for a journey to search for the truth, locked up under our reality. Ultimately, this is the act of going on a journey to become reality, in order to restore it. But, then, isn't this the role that poems have always played? It is clear to me that, at some point, as poems become more and more helpless in the face of reality's fragmentation, instead of restoring and becoming reality, they have accepted the fact that poetry is nothing but a helplessness.

To look at this matter from another perspective, for poems to become "something" in reality on their own is a step toward overcoming the utilitarian framework about their usefulness or uselessness. The question of poems becoming "something" in reality is based on the understanding that poems are living organisms, and that, like all living organisms, they are born, move, and die. To prove this point, we'll certainly need deeper thoughts and languages, as well as writing concrete poems. But what's most important is that the agent of such poems, that is, the poet, should be able to accept such an idea with their minds and souls. This is because embodying poems as works of art is only possible by the agent writing it, and because a poet does not exist outside or above reality.

Once poems become deeply embedded in reality, by becoming its components, their dreams can become no longer utopian. Rather, by participating in relationships in reality, poems achieve a new reality. That is, for a poem to succeed in becoming a component of reality means the poem has already created a new reality. Ironically, this is possible only based on grand imagination, which goes back in civilization. Modern science and technology cannot act as companions in the creation of a new reality that poems engage. And it goes without saying that artificial intelligence cannot write poems that can become "something" in reality. Therefore, there is no need for such poems to fear artificial intelligence.

What matters is not this kind of argument or logical thesis, but for poems of this nature to be born as works of art. I dare to claim that the capability of poems to oppose our extremely elaborate modern capitalist civilization becomes materialized at the moment when a poem becomes "something" in reality. And the moment when these realistic events, in which poems bloom, occur, we can call that moment a new time.

In retrospect, late poet Kim Su-yeong revealed clues to this kind of understanding of poems. "A poetic understanding is the discovery of a new truth (which is a new reality) and the discovery of a new eye and angle to see objects," he said in his "February 1967 Poetry Review: Poetic Understanding and Newness." Although he explicitly mentioned only "discovery" in this writing, he actually went further in his understanding, and we can glimpse it in the phrase in which he reflects on his poems through comparing them with his mother's belief and manual labor: "I wonder when I will do writing like my mother's hand—I have a long way to go." (from Kim Su-yeong, "Against Poetry")

It is because of the dire reality that has now befallen us that poems must attain the "creation" of a new truth. Although, in any period those who bear it feel their reality to be the heaviest, the reality we are confronting today appears too heavy to be borne by the same past level of despair and grief. Although the world today appears headed toward a new form, this new world is approaching us while at the same time destroying our minds and souls. Yet, as minds and souls are closely related to our physical ability, taking care of our minds and souls can be accomplished through taking care of our physicality. Modern capitalist civilization, which conditions our current way of life, can continue to exist only by degenerating our physical abilities. We are now living entirely separate from the earth, and all lives have become raw materials for or components of profit.

As this is the condition of our reality, it is impossible for us to manage our lives soundly. However, reality does not change simply because of our will to change it. Nor is reality moving according to our thoughts. On the contrary, reality can deteriorate despite our intentions. Similarly, although poems can change reality, we must acknowledge the contemporary situation in which poems can deteriorate it even through the slightest misstep. The contemporary time is not one when our side and their side can be clearly distinguished. Nevertheless, we are not really facing the world entirely different from before either.

Therefore, poems should go beyond existing boundaries and accept the innumerable beings that now exist as undeniable reality, so that poems can begin from that reality again. I am not arguing that we should use our reality as a host or accept it as our fate. On the contrary, the work of exploring the truth that our current reality has locked up—I believe this is the work of creating a new reality. Like all creations, this one is not play. It is more like anguished labor that we engage in, after reaching an inevitable limit or a wall, in order to delay or break through it even a little. However, even if poems succeed in creating a new reality, it's not their ultimate goal. The new reality is only leading us to gusty fields. But this is not at all a tragedy, but rather the work of regaining lost laughter.

Laughter acquired during play and laughter acquired through anguished labor have different existential foundations. Unlike the former, the latter is the key to the door of a new truth. In other words, the former is just nihil, while the latter is a will to newly define being, the physical ability of the agent writing poems. Therefore, creating poems as an act of creating a new truth is more like a dynamic action of a body. Further, this action enables a movement in which poems become "something" in reality on their own. That is, a poet's role is to enable a poem to arise on its own and carry out movements, and thus a poet is a medium to reveal poems in language by being possessed by them. Yet poems are not something a transcendental being bestows upon us from above, but are like the lightning created during the clash of concrete real lives. In order to gladly enjoy an electric shock from that lightning, what physical abilities should a poet possess?

COMMENTARY

K
POET

Toward a Small and Dark Place

Moon Jong-pil (Literary critic)

The situation now is that our existence itself will crumble if we commit adultery with science and technology. I feel a serious sense of crisis. Then is there a solution? Finding an answer to that question does not seem to be my role. If I must "stare at" something, I'll stare at science and technology approaching like a monster. This is not a plan. My soul cannot stand it more by the day. I must fight them in order to live. And, as long as I am alive, I'll continue to write poems. *

* Hwang Gyu-gwan, "Sometimes Being in Pain Becomes a Great Fight (5)," *Webzine Munhwa Da*, Feb 5-9, 2020.

To poet Hwang Gyu-gwan , a soul is very important.[*] To him, a soul is related to what is upright and just. It makes him remain standing and be alive. Then what does the soul look like to him? Criticizing the structure of technological capitalism, which degenerates the ability of our bodies, he argues that we should take care of "minds and souls."[**] According to him, advanced civilization prevents our souls from being free. So he is not satisfied with this place he is living in. He does not like the eyes that reduce everything to something exchangeable, rather than respecting a warmth touching our skin. Standing in the midst of the current, posthuman time, he simply stares at people's faces. Although the development of ever-renewed technological civilization may not be negated, he wants to discuss the gaps in this civ-

* Hwang Gyu-gwan has written poems consistently and for a long time. He has published six books of poems and this book will be his seventh.

** See "Poet's Note."

ilization through the traces of previous times that human beings have borne for a long time.

This attitude is revealed in his poetry. He believes that poetry is created through the combination of a sound mind and a soul. From his perspective, if a soul is murky, poems will resemble its murky form. If our soul is clear and transparent, our poems will resemble its clear and transparent color. Based on this belief, he trains his soul. Also, as mind and soul are closely related to skin, poetic form is a synonym for life. Thus, his poetics is the poetics of an honest body.

However, his wish is not easily fulfilled. The poet's soul does not seem to find vitality in the present. Then what does the soul he wants to resemble look like? While an "enormous soul" ("The True Identity of Waves") is what he wishes to resemble, a "hardened soul" ("Jujube Tree") is what should be discarded. So a beneficial soul allows the speaker to recover his senses by shaking him and his hardened body "with a creaking sound" ("Tiger Swallowtail"). The speaker then looks up at the sky and clutches his small hands. It is a new beginning. This kind of repetition and renewal that makes him not grow worn-out is his writing. However, he does not pursue only an enormous soul. The soul he wants to resemble is in a low and humble place. It is similar to the trace of the half moon that cannot be found these days because "the world had become too bright" ("Half Moon"). It is the skin that has not been touched because of our busy daily lives. He lodges his hope in trivial and affectionate souls.

Nevertheless, his soul is now being clouded. It is difficult to find the half moon in the city where he lives because of the bright lights. As it is hard to find the being that raised his body whenever he ran into difficulties, it is also difficult to find a place for him to lean on. The cause of this situation is not entirely outside. He is to blame as well, because he hasn't always maintained a tension. At this point, he has to think of physical time. He cannot move his body like before. Perhaps a sadness from this situation pushed the soul backward. This is why he is reminded of the absence of "souls" from flowers ("There Is Nothing But Flowers"), and gropes for the traces of wholesome "souls" ("A Pickaxe and a Donkey") while touching a hoe. This might lead some readers to think that the poet's body is in danger. But this supposition is premature. Rather, we should consider that he is on a threshold.

It is a poet's fate to renew himself and plod along a new road, although he is bearing a worn-out body. It is a poet's way to fight against a wall until his fingernails are crushed, even when he runs into a wall and desperately stamps his feet. The soul he has been embracing is now searching for a new road. The footsteps of a "soul that has transferred to a different time" ("Winter Valley") is preparing for a leap. He is looking for a new road while wandering alone at what seems a dead-end. As he has arrived at the end too early, he might not be able to exercise his might fully. However, he again musters his strength. Looking back at the road he has taken so far, he is also staring at the road about to be taken. The poems related to a road in this book talk about this point. Then what is the "road taken" and what is it to him?

Two poems related to a road are impressive. They describe the road about to be taken in detail. Reading these poems, readers can presume the atmosphere of the road the poet wanted to take. The poet says, "A road newly taken/Is a road always taken for the first time" and "the road newly taken wants/To offer me a different kind of darkness." ("Toward the Direction of Daybreak") He also says, "The road not taken is always/An invisible road" and "A road where aches from a daylong hoeing/Are crawling all over your body." ("The Road Not Taken") Considering these traces of the road, it is not hard to presume that he is now only temporarily withdrawn, but will surely rise up again soon. He is never going to give up. He will confidently write poems again, just as he did during his confident youth.

On reflection, this attitude of the poet teaches us a lesson: It is more meaningful to not give up, even when you stand at the impasse, and to continue mustering the will to take the new road. Rather, what's not desirable is an attitude that is unable to question the road that has been taken. Therefore, the poet's soul is still healthy. Then how will the poet stand up? He will agonize over which possibilities to choose among innumerable ones within himself. As his reader, I find this point the most interesting. Let's now conclude.

At a crossroads, the poet chooses traces of his

youth. He returns to an earlier time, grabs the moments of brightness there, and regroups. "Daytime Moon" shows this. Let's reveal the landscape described in it. They is the jujube tree in front of the house, a mother's sigh, the gust of yesterday, the spring water he happened to encounter in the forest, a rock standing alone, the sunlight touching the river, grains of sand on the riverbed, and the lonely moon in the sky. The poet clearly wants to recover what he felt during his youth. This effort helps him endure the here and now.

However, we cannot unconditionally praise this approach. The traces of his youth are illusions that cannot be recovered here and now. It can also be read as an effort to return to the past in order to avoid present danger. It also seems to reflect the anxiety that the poetic subject cannot avoid feeling as time passes. The anxiety creates illusions and reproduces distorted intentions. Although this approach is not negative, it might be a reflection of the fact that human beings cannot help becoming weaker. Hwang is currently standing at the crossroads. He is shivering a little.

Yet we don't see that he lets go of his perseverance. We can confirm his criticism of civilization in poems like "A Time of a Precipice," "Let's Set the Forests Free," and "Shadows." The voice saying, "Let's set them[the forests] free from humans," and the act of protest against civil servants who are pruning tree branches are gestures of resistance against contemporary civilization harassing the earth, testifying to the vitality of his soul.

His conscience is still alive. Because of this, we can daydream the following: Although he asks about the road not yet taken, he is also unconsciously presenting his answer to it: the fight against civilization. The possibilities are not outside--the poet has been cherishing it in his heart.

He is preparing for a renewed leap through a language with bone, one his "mother can understand" ("The Voice of a Creek"). Although he "might become poverty, might become solitude,/Might become raindrops," ("Let's Write Poems") he will not stop writing poems. In search of language that "descend[s] in my heart" ("Spring Snow"), he will continue to wander bravely in his neighborhood, taverns, and the traces of footsteps left by his neighbors.

We end up cheering naturally for the road he's taking. His life is also ours. And the cheers we send him are cheers for ourselves, too. Therefore, let's all rise up again. Let's "become a little smaller" and "much darker, like a valley." ("Cremation")

WHAT THEY SAY ABOUT HWANG GYU-GWAN

We may now call him 'the priest of natural lyricism'. While both succeeding and overcoming Kim Su-yeong's fierce language and thought, Hwang Gyu-gwan vividly shows for us how the difficulty and peacefulness of life, labor and rest, the past and present, eternity and a moment, and epic and lyric poetry, all worked together.

Yu Seong-ho, *Changbi*, 2020

"A poet is a person who brings pain and discomfort to the reader. They are not a priest leading us to a state of enlightenment, but a whistleblower uncovering truth, and clashing with the world. Therefore, a poet is always lonely. Let's end this 'time of fire' with poet Hwang Gyu-gwan. Let's not go along with the aggressive speed of capitalism."

Park Hyeong-jun, *Literary Criticism Today*, 2020

K-POET
Tiger Swallowtail

Written by Hwang Gyu-gwan
Translated by Jeon Seung-hee
Published by ASIA Publishers
Address 445, Hoedong-gil, Paju-si, Gyeonggi-do, Korea
Homepage Address www.bookasia.org
Tel (8231).955.7958
Fax (8231).955.7956
ISBN 979-11-5662-317-5 (set) | 979-11-5662-548-3 (04810)

First published in Korea by ASIA Publishers 2021

This book is published with the support of the Literature Translation Institute of Korea (LTI Korea).